Order Tracker Notebook For

Business Name _____

Address _____

_____

Book NO.:

_____

Continued From Book NO.:

_____

Start Date:

/   /

_____

copyright © 2022   By   Luju Golden Press

Order form

Order No.: _____

Order Date : ___ / ___ / ___

Customer Details

Name : _____

Address : _____

_____

Email : _____ @ _____ Phone : _____

Order Details - Description	Quantity	Unit Price	Total

Started ☐

Done ☐

Shipped ☐

Notes _____
_____
_____
_____

Shipping Details

Price

Shipping Method : _____

Date Shipped : _____

Tracking# : _____

Date : _____

Subtotal : _____

Tax : _____

Shipping : _____

Discount : _____

Total _____

Order form

Customer Details

Name : _____

Address : _____

_____

Email : _____ @ _____ Phone : _____

Order Details - Description	Quantity	Unit Price	Total

Started ☐

Done ☐

Shipped ☐

Notes _____
_____
_____
_____

Shipping Details

Price

Shipping Method : _____

Date Shipped : _____

Tracking# : _____

Date : _____

Subtotal : _____

Tax : _____

Shipping : _____

Discount : _____

Total _____

Order form

Order No.: _____

Order Date : ___ / ___ / ___

Customer Details

Name : _____

Address : _____

_____

Email : _____ @ _____ Phone : _____

Order Details - Description	Quantity	Unit Price	Total

Started ☐

Done ☐

Shipped ☐

Notes _____
_____
_____

Shipping Details

Price

Shipping Method : _____

Date Shipped : _____

Tracking# : _____

Date : _____

Subtotal : _____

Tax : _____

Shipping : _____

Discount : _____

Total _____

Order form

Order No.: _____

Order Date : ___/___/___

Customer Details

Name : _____

Address : _____

_____

Email : _____ @ _____ Phone : _____

Order Details - Description	Quantity	Unit Price	Total

Started ☐

Done ☐

Shipped ☐

Notes _____
_____
_____
_____

Shipping Details

Shipping Method : _____

Date Shipped : _____

Tracking# : _____

Date : _____

Price

Subtotal : _____

Tax : _____

Shipping : _____

Discount : _____

Total _____

Order form

Order No.: _____

Order Date : _____ / _____ / _____

Customer Details

Name : _____

Address : _____

_____

Email : _____ @ _____ Phone : _____

Order Details - Description	Quantity	Unit Price	Total

Started ☐

Done ☐

Shipped ☐

Notes _____
_____
_____

Shipping Details

Shipping Method : _____

Date Shipped : _____

Tracking# : _____

Date : _____

Price

Subtotal : _____

Tax : _____

Shipping : _____

Discount : _____

Total _____

Order form

Order No.: _____

Order Date : ____/____/____

Customer Details

Name : _____

Address : _____

_____

Email : _____ @ _____ Phone : _____

Order Details - Description	Quantity	Unit Price	Total

Started ☐

Done ☐

Shipped ☐

Notes _____
_____
_____
_____

Shipping Details

Price

Shipping Method : _____

Date Shipped : _____

Tracking# : _____

Date : _____

Subtotal : _____

Tax : _____

Shipping : _____

Discount : _____

Total

Order form

Order No.: _____

Order Date : ___ / ___ / ___

Customer Details

Name : _____

Address : _____

_____

Email : _____ @ _____   Phone : _____

Order Details - Description	Quantity	Unit Price	Total

Started ☐

Done ☐

Shipped ☐

Notes _____
_____
_____
_____

Shipping Details

Shipping Method : _____

Date Shipped : _____

Tracking# : _____

Date : _____

Price

Subtotal : _____

Tax : _____

Shipping : _____

Discount : _____

Total : _____

Order form

Customer Details

Name : _____

Address : _____

_____

Email : _____ @ _____   Phone : _____

Order Details - Description	Quantity	Unit Price	Total

Started ☐   Notes _____

Done ☐   _____

Shipped ☐   _____

_____

Shipping Details

Price

Shipping Method : _____

Date Shipped : _____

Tracking# : _____

Date : _____

Subtotal : _____

Tax : _____

Shipping : _____

Discount : _____

Total _____

Order form

Order No.: _____

Order Date : ___ / ___ / ___

Customer Details

Name : _____

Address : _____

_____

Email : _____ @ _____ Phone : _____

Order Details - Description	Quantity	Unit Price	Total

Started ☐

Done ☐

Shipped ☐

Notes _____
_____
_____
_____

Shipping Details

Price

Shipping Method : _____

Date Shipped : _____

Tracking# : _____

Date : _____

Subtotal : _____

Tax : _____

Shipping : _____

Discount : _____

Total _____

Order form

Order No.: _____

Order Date : ___ / ___ / ___

Customer Details

Name : _____

Address : _____

_____

Email : _____ @ _____ Phone : _____

Order Details - Description	Quantity	Unit Price	Total

Started ☐

Done ☐

Shipped ☐

Notes _____
_____
_____
_____

Shipping Details

Price

Shipping Method : _____

Date Shipped : _____

Tracking# : _____

Date : _____

Subtotal : _____

Tax : _____

Shipping : _____

Discount : _____

Total _____

Order form

Order No.: _____

Order Date : ___ / ___ / ___

Customer Details

Name : _____

Address : _____

_____

Email : _____ @ _____   Phone : _____

Order Details - Description	Quantity	Unit Price	Total

Started ☐

Done ☐

Shipped ☐

Notes _____
_____
_____

Shipping Details

Shipping Method : _____

Date Shipped : _____

Tracking# : _____

Date : _____

Price

Subtotal : _____

Tax : _____

Shipping : _____

Discount : _____

Total _____

Order form

Order No.: _____

Order Date : ___ / ___ / ___

Customer Details

Name : _____

Address : _____

_____

Email : _____ @ _____ Phone : _____

Order Details - Description	Quantity	Unit Price	Total

Started ☐

Done ☐

Shipped ☐

Notes _____
_____
_____
_____

Shipping Details

Price

Shipping Method : _____

Date Shipped : _____

Tracking# : _____

Date : _____

Subtotal : _____

Tax : _____

Shipping : _____

Discount : _____

Total

Order form

Customer Details

Name : _____

Address : _____

_____

Email : _____ @ _____ Phone : _____

Order Details - Description	Quantity	Unit Price	Total

Started ☐

Done ☐

Shipped ☐

Notes _____
_____
_____
_____

Shipping Details

Price

Shipping Method : _____

Date Shipped : _____

Tracking# : _____

Date : _____

Subtotal : _____

Tax : _____

Shipping : _____

Discount : _____

Total _____

Order form

Order No.: _____

Order Date : ___ / ___ / ___

Customer Details

Name : _____

Address : _____

_____

Email : _____ @ _____   Phone : _____

Order Details - Description	Quantity	Unit Price	Total

Started ◻

Done ◻

Shipped ◻

Notes _____
_____
_____
_____

Shipping Details

Price

Shipping Method : _____

Date Shipped : _____

Tracking# : _____

Date : _____

Subtotal : _____

Tax : _____

Shipping : _____

Discount : _____

Total _____

Order form

Order No.: _____

Order Date : ___ / ___ / ___

Customer Details

Name : _____

Address : _____

_____

Email : _____ @ _____ Phone : _____

Order Details - Description	Quantity	Unit Price	Total

Started ☐

Done ☐

Shipped ☐

Notes _____
_____
_____
_____

Shipping Details

Shipping Method : _____

Date Shipped : _____

Tracking# : _____

Date : _____

Price

Subtotal : _____

Tax : _____

Shipping : _____

Discount : _____

Total _____

Order form

Order No.: _____

Order Date : ___ / ___ / ___

Customer Details

Name : _____

Address : _____

_____

Email : _____ @ _____   Phone : _____

Order Details - Description	Quantity	Unit Price	Total

Started ☐

Done ☐

Shipped ☐

Notes _____
_____
_____
_____

Shipping Details

Shipping Method : _____

Date Shipped : _____

Tracking# : _____

Date : _____

Price

Subtotal : _____

Tax : _____

Shipping : _____

Discount : _____

Total _____

Order form

Order No.: _____

Order Date : ___/___/___

Customer Details

Name : _____

Address : _____

_____

Email : _____ @ _____ Phone : _____

Order Details - Description	Quantity	Unit Price	Total

Started ☐

Done ☐

Shipped ☐

Notes _____

_____

_____

_____

Shipping Details

Shipping Method : _____

Date Shipped : _____

Tracking# : _____

Date : _____

Price

Subtotal : _____

Tax : _____

Shipping : _____

Discount : _____

Total _____

Order form

Customer Details

Name : _____

Address : _____

_____

Email : _____ @ _____ Phone : _____

Order Details - Description	Quantity	Unit Price	Total

Started ☐

Done ☐

Shipped ☐

Notes _____
_____
_____
_____

Shipping Details

Price

Shipping Method : _____

Date Shipped : _____

Tracking# : _____

Date : _____

Subtotal : _____

Tax : _____

Shipping : _____

Discount : _____

Total _____

Order form

Order No.: _____

Order Date : ___ / ___ / ___

Customer Details

Name : _____

Address : _____

_____

Email : _____ @ _____ Phone : _____

Order Details - Description	Quantity	Unit Price	Total

Started ☐

Done ☐

Shipped ☐

Notes _____
_____
_____

Shipping Details

Shipping Method : _____

Date Shipped : _____

Tracking# : _____

Date : _____

Price

Subtotal : _____

Tax : _____

Shipping : _____

Discount : _____

Total _____

Order form

Order No.: _____

Order Date : ___ / ___ / ___

Customer Details

Name : _____

Address : _____

_____

Email : _____ @ _____ Phone : _____

Order Details - Description	Quantity	Unit Price	Total

Started ☐

Done ☐

Shipped ☐

Notes _____

_____

_____

Shipping Details

Shipping Method : _____

Date Shipped : _____

Tracking# : _____

Date : _____

Price

Subtotal : _____

Tax : _____

Shipping : _____

Discount : _____

Total _____

Order form

Order No.: _____

Order Date : ___ / ___ / ___

Customer Details

Name : _____

Address : _____

_____

Email : _____ @ _____ Phone : _____

Order Details - Description	Quantity	Unit Price	Total

Started ☐

Done ☐

Shipped ☐

Notes _____
_____
_____
_____

Shipping Details

Price

Shipping Method : _____

Date Shipped : _____

Tracking# : _____

Date : _____

Subtotal : _____

Tax : _____

Shipping : _____

Discount : _____

Total _____

Order form

Order No.: _____

Order Date : ___ / ___ / ___

Customer Details

Name : _____

Address : _____

_____

Email : _____ @ _____ Phone : _____

Order Details - Description	Quantity	Unit Price	Total

Started ☐

Done ☐

Shipped ☐

Notes _____
_____
_____
_____

Shipping Details

Price

Shipping Method : _____

Date Shipped : _____

Tracking# : _____

Date : _____

Subtotal : _____

Tax : _____

Shipping : _____

Discount : _____

Total _____

Order form

Customer Details

Name : _____

Address : _____

_____

Email : _____ @ _____   Phone : _____

Order Details - Description	Quantity	Unit Price	Total

Started ☐
Done ☐
Shipped ☐

Notes _____
_____
_____
_____

Shipping Details

Shipping Method : _____

Date Shipped : _____

Tracking# : _____

Date : _____

Price

Subtotal : _____

Tax : _____

Shipping : _____

Discount : _____

Total _____

Order form

Order No.: _____

Order Date : ___ / ___ / ___

Customer Details

Name : _____

Address : _____

_____

Email : _____ @ _____ Phone : _____

Order Details - Description	Quantity	Unit Price	Total

Started ☐

Done ☐

Shipped ☐

Notes _____
_____
_____
_____

Shipping Details

Price

Shipping Method : _____

Date Shipped : _____

Tracking# : _____

Date : _____

Subtotal : _____

Tax : _____

Shipping : _____

Discount : _____

Total _____

Order form

Order No.: _____

Order Date : ___ / ___ / ___

Customer Details

Name : _____

Address : _____

_____

Email : _____ @ _____ Phone : _____

Order Details - Description	Quantity	Unit Price	Total

Started ☐

Done ☐

Shipped ☐

Notes _____
_____
_____
_____

Shipping Details

Price

Shipping Method : _____

Date Shipped : _____

Tracking# : _____

Date : _____

Subtotal : _____

Tax : _____

Shipping : _____

Discount : _____

Total _____

Order form

Order No.: _____

Order Date : __/__/__

Customer Details

Name : _____

Address : _____

_____

Email : _____ @ _____ Phone : _____

Order Details - Description	Quantity	Unit Price	Total

Started ◻

Done ◻

Shipped ◻

Notes _____
_____
_____
_____

Shipping Details

Price

Shipping Method : _____

Date Shipped : _____

Tracking# : _____

Date : _____

Subtotal : _____

Tax : _____

Shipping : _____

Discount : _____

Total _____

Order form

Order No.: _____

Order Date : ___ / ___ / ___

Customer Details

Name : _____

Address : _____

_____

Email : _____ @ _____   Phone : _____

Order Details - Description	Quantity	Unit Price	Total

Started ☐

Done ☐

Shipped ☐

Notes _____
_____
_____
_____

Shipping Details

Price

Shipping Method : _____

Date Shipped : _____

Tracking# : _____

Date : _____

Subtotal : _____

Tax : _____

Shipping : _____

Discount : _____

Total _____

Order form

Order No.: _____

Order Date : ___ / ___ / ___

Customer Details

Name : _____

Address : _____

_____

Email : _____ @ _____ Phone : _____

Order Details - Description	Quantity	Unit Price	Total

Started ☐

Done ☐

Shipped ☐

Notes _____
_____
_____

Shipping Details

Price

Shipping Method : _____

Date Shipped : _____

Tracking# : _____

Date : _____

Subtotal : _____

Tax : _____

Shipping : _____

Discount : _____

Total _____

Order form

Order No.: _____

Order Date : ___ / ___ / ___

Customer Details

Name : _____

Address : _____

_____

Email : _____ @ _____   Phone : _____

Order Details - Description	Quantity	Unit Price	Total

Started ☐

Done ☐

Shipped ☐

Notes _____
_____
_____
_____

Shipping Details

Price

Shipping Method : _____

Date Shipped : _____

Tracking# : _____

Date : _____

Subtotal : _____

Tax : _____

Shipping : _____

Discount : _____

Total _____

Order form

Order No.: _____

Order Date : ___ / ___ / ___

Customer Details

Name : _____

Address : _____

_____

Email : _____ @ _____ Phone : _____

Order Details - Description	Quantity	Unit Price	Total

Started ☐

Done ☐

Shipped ☐

Notes _____
_____
_____
_____

Shipping Details

Shipping Method : _____

Date Shipped : _____

Tracking# : _____

Date : _____

Price

Subtotal : _____

Tax : _____

Shipping : _____

Discount : _____

Total _____

Order form

Order No.: _____

Order Date : _____ / _____ / _____

Customer Details

Name : _____

Address : _____

_____

Email : _____ @ _____ Phone : _____

Order Details - Description	Quantity	Unit Price	Total

Started ☐

Done ☐

Shipped ☐

Notes _____

_____

_____

_____

Shipping Details

Shipping Method : _____

Date Shipped : _____

Tracking# : _____

Date : _____

Price

Subtotal : _____

Tax : _____

Shipping : _____

Discount : _____

Total _____

Order form

Order No.: _____

Order Date : ___ / ___ / ___

Customer Details

Name : _____

Address : _____

_____

Email : _____ @ _____ Phone : _____

Order Details - Description	Quantity	Unit Price	Total

Started ☐

Done ☐

Shipped ☐

Notes _____
_____
_____
_____

Shipping Details

Price

Shipping Method : _____

Date Shipped : _____

Tracking# : _____

Date : _____

Subtotal : _____

Tax : _____

Shipping : _____

Discount : _____

Total _____

Order form

Order No.: _____

Order Date : ____ / ____ / ____

Customer Details

Name : _____

Address : _____

_____

Email : _____ @ _____ Phone : _____

Order Details - Description	Quantity	Unit Price	Total

Started ☐

Done ☐

Shipped ☐

Notes _____
_____
_____
_____

Shipping Details

Shipping Method : _____

Date Shipped : _____

Tracking# : _____

Date : _____

Price

Subtotal : _____

Tax : _____

Shipping : _____

Discount : _____

Total _____

Order form

Order No.: _____

Order Date : ____ / ____ / ____

Customer Details

Name : _____

Address : _____

_____

Email : _____ @ _____ Phone : _____

Order Details - Description	Quantity	Unit Price	Total

Started ☐

Done ☐

Shipped ☐

Notes _____
_____
_____
_____

Shipping Details

Price

Shipping Method : _____

Date Shipped : _____

Tracking# : _____

Date : _____

Subtotal : _____

Tax : _____

Shipping : _____

Discount : _____

Total _____

Order form

Order No.: _____

Order Date : ____/____/____

Customer Details

Name : _____

Address : _____

_____

Email : _____ @ _____ Phone : _____

Order Details - Description	Quantity	Unit Price	Total

Started ☐

Done ☐

Shipped ☐

Notes _____
_____
_____
_____

Shipping Details

Price

Shipping Method : _____

Date Shipped : _____

Tracking# : _____

Date : _____

Subtotal : _____

Tax : _____

Shipping : _____

Discount : _____

Total _____

Order form

Order No.: _____
Order Date : ___/___/___

Customer Details

Name : _____

Address : _____

_____

Email : _____ @ _____ Phone : _____

Order Details - Description	Quantity	Unit Price	Total

Started ☐

Done ☐

Shipped ☐

Notes _____
_____
_____
_____

Shipping Details

Shipping Method : _____

Date Shipped : _____

Tracking# : _____

Date : _____

Price

Subtotal : _____

Tax : _____

Shipping : _____

Discount : _____

Total _____

Order form

Order No.: _____

Order Date : ___/___/___

Customer Details

Name : _____

Address : _____

_____

Email : _____ @ _____ Phone : _____

Order Details - Description	Quantity	Unit Price	Total

Started ☐

Done ☐

Shipped ☐

Notes _____

_____

_____

_____

Shipping Details

Shipping Method : _____

Date Shipped : _____

Tracking# : _____

Date : _____

Price

Subtotal : _____

Tax : _____

Shipping : _____

Discount : _____

Total _____

Order form

Order No.: _____

Order Date : ___ / ___ / ___

Customer Details

Name : _____

Address : _____

_____

Email : _____ @ _____ Phone : _____

Order Details - Description	Quantity	Unit Price	Total

Started ☐

Done ☐

Shipped ☐

Notes _____
_____
_____
_____

Shipping Details

Shipping Method : _____

Date Shipped : _____

Tracking# : _____

Date : _____

Price

Subtotal : _____

Tax : _____

Shipping : _____

Discount : _____

Total _____

Order form

Order No.: _____

Order Date : ____ / ____ / ____

Customer Details

Name : _____

Address : _____

_____

Email : _____ @ _____ Phone : _____

Order Details - Description	Quantity	Unit Price	Total

Started ☐

Done ☐

Shipped ☐

Notes _____
_____
_____

Shipping Details

Price

Shipping Method : _____

Date Shipped : _____

Tracking# : _____

Date : _____

Subtotal : _____

Tax : _____

Shipping : _____

Discount : _____

Total _____

Order form

Customer Details

Name : _____

Address : _____

_____

Email : _____ @ _____ Phone : _____

Order Details - Description	Quantity	Unit Price	Total

Started ☐

Done ☐

Shipped ☐

Notes _____

_____

_____

_____

Shipping Details

Price

Shipping Method : _____

Date Shipped : _____

Tracking# : _____

Date : _____

Subtotal : _____

Tax : _____

Shipping : _____

Discount : _____

Total _____

Order form

Customer Details

Name : _____

Address : _____

_____

Email : _____ @ _____ Phone : _____

Order Details - Description	Quantity	Unit Price	Total

Started ☐

Done ☐

Shipped ☐

Notes _____
_____
_____

Shipping Details

Price

Shipping Method : _____

Date Shipped : _____

Tracking# : _____

Date : _____

Subtotal : _____

Tax : _____

Shipping : _____

Discount : _____

Total _____

Order form

Order No.: _____

Order Date : ___ / ___ / ___

Customer Details

Name : _____

Address : _____

_____

Email : _____ @ _____ Phone : _____

Order Details - Description	Quantity	Unit Price	Total

Started ☐

Done ☐

Shipped ☐

Notes _____
_____
_____
_____

Shipping Details

Shipping Method : _____

Date Shipped : _____

Tracking# : _____

Date : _____

Price

Subtotal : _____

Tax : _____

Shipping : _____

Discount : _____

Total _____

Order form

Order No.: _____

Order Date : ____ / ____ / ____

Customer Details

Name : _____

Address : _____

_____

Email : _____ @ _____ Phone : _____

Order Details - Description	Quantity	Unit Price	Total

Started ☐

Done ☐

Shipped ☐

Notes _____
_____
_____
_____

Shipping Details

Price

Shipping Method : _____

Date Shipped : _____

Tracking# : _____

Date : _____

Subtotal : _____

Tax : _____

Shipping : _____

Discount : _____

Total _____

Order form

Order No.: _____

Order Date : ___ / ___ / ___

Customer Details

Name : _____

Address : _____

_____

Email : _____ @ _____ Phone : _____

Order Details - Description	Quantity	Unit Price	Total

Started ☐

Done ☐

Shipped ☐

Notes _____
_____
_____
_____

Shipping Details

Shipping Method : _____

Date Shipped : _____

Tracking# : _____

Date : _____

Price

Subtotal : _____

Tax : _____

Shipping : _____

Discount : _____

Total _____

Order form

Order No.: _____

Order Date : ___ / ___ / ___

Customer Details

Name : _____

Address : _____

_____

Email : _____ @ _____   Phone : _____

Order Details - Description	Quantity	Unit Price	Total

Started ☐

Done ☐

Shipped ☐

Notes _____
_____
_____
_____

Shipping Details

Shipping Method : _____

Date Shipped : _____

Tracking# : _____

Date : _____

Price

Subtotal : _____

Tax : _____

Shipping : _____

Discount : _____

Total _____

Order form

Order No.: _____

Order Date : ___ / ___ / ___

Customer Details

Name : _____

Address : _____

_____

Email : _____ @ _____ Phone : _____

Order Details - Description	Quantity	Unit Price	Total

Started ☐

Done ☐

Shipped ☐

Notes _____
_____
_____
_____

Shipping Details

Shipping Method : _____

Date Shipped : _____

Tracking# : _____

Date : _____

Price

Subtotal : _____

Tax : _____

Shipping : _____

Discount : _____

Total _____

Order form

Order No.: _____

Order Date : ___ / ___ / ___

Customer Details

Name : _____

Address : _____

_____

Email : _____ @ _____ Phone : _____

Order Details - Description	Quantity	Unit Price	Total

Started ☐

Done ☐

Shipped ☐

Notes _____

_____

_____

Shipping Details

Price

Shipping Method : _____

Date Shipped : _____

Tracking# : _____

Date : _____

Subtotal : _____

Tax : _____

Shipping : _____

Discount : _____

Total _____

Order form

Order No.: _____

Order Date : ___/___/___

Customer Details

Name : _____

Address : _____

_____

Email : _____ @ _____   Phone : _____

Order Details - Description	Quantity	Unit Price	Total

Started ☐

Done ☐

Shipped ☐

Notes _____

_____

_____

Shipping Details

Price

Shipping Method : _____

Date Shipped : _____

Tracking# : _____

Date : _____

Subtotal : _____

Tax : _____

Shipping : _____

Discount : _____

Total _____

Order form

Customer Details

Name : _____

Address : _____

_____

Email : _____ @ _____ Phone : _____

Order Details - Description	Quantity	Unit Price	Total

Started ☐

Done ☐

Shipped ☐

Notes _____
_____
_____
_____

Shipping Details

Shipping Method : _____

Date Shipped : _____

Tracking# : _____

Date : _____

Price

Subtotal : _____

Tax : _____

Shipping : _____

Discount : _____

Total : _____

Order form

Order No.: _____

Order Date : ___ / ___ / ___

Customer Details

Name : _____

Address : _____

_____

Email : _____ @ _____   Phone : _____

Order Details - Description	Quantity	Unit Price	Total

Started ☐   Notes _____

Done ☐   _____

Shipped ☐   _____

Shipping Details

Price

Shipping Method : _____

Date Shipped : _____

Tracking# : _____

Date : _____

Subtotal : _____

Tax : _____

Shipping : _____

Discount : _____

Total _____

Order form

Order No.: _____

Order Date : ___ / ___ / ___

Customer Details

Name : _____

Address : _____

_____

Email : _____ @ _____ Phone : _____

Order Details - Description	Quantity	Unit Price	Total

Started ☐

Done ☐

Shipped ☐

Notes _____
_____
_____
_____

Shipping Details

Shipping Method : _____

Date Shipped : _____

Tracking# : _____

Date : _____

Price

Subtotal : _____

Tax : _____

Shipping : _____

Discount : _____

Total _____

Order form

Order No.: _____

Order Date : ____ / ____ / ____

Customer Details

Name : _____

Address : _____

_____

Email : _____ @ _____ Phone : _____

Order Details - Description	Quantity	Unit Price	Total

Started ☐

Done ☐

Shipped ☐

Notes _____
_____
_____
_____

Shipping Details

Price

Shipping Method : _____

Date Shipped : _____

Tracking# : _____

Date : _____

Subtotal : _____

Tax : _____

Shipping : _____

Discount : _____

Total _____

Order form

Order No.: _____
Order Date : ___ / ___ / ___

Customer Details

Name : _____

Address : _____

_____

Email : _____ @ _____ Phone : _____

Order Details - Description	Quantity	Unit Price	Total

Started ☐

Done ☐

Shipped ☐

Notes _____
_____
_____
_____

Shipping Details

Price

Shipping Method : _____

Date Shipped : _____

Tracking# : _____

Date : _____

Subtotal : _____

Tax : _____

Shipping : _____

Discount : _____

Total _____

Order form

Order No.: _____

Order Date : ___ / ___ / ___

Customer Details

Name : _____

Address : _____

_____

Email : _____ @ _____ Phone : _____

Order Details - Description	Quantity	Unit Price	Total

Started ☐

Done ☐

Shipped ☐

Notes _____
_____
_____
_____

Shipping Details

Price

Shipping Method : _____

Date Shipped : _____

Tracking# : _____

Date : _____

Subtotal : _____

Tax : _____

Shipping : _____

Discount : _____

Total _____

Order form

Customer Details

Name : _____

Address : _____

_____

Email : _____ @ _____ Phone : _____

Order Details - Description	Quantity	Unit Price	Total

Started ☐

Done ☐

Shipped ☐

Notes _____
_____
_____
_____

Shipping Details

Price

Shipping Method : _____

Date Shipped : _____

Tracking# : _____

Date : _____

Subtotal : _____

Tax : _____

Shipping : _____

Discount : _____

Total _____

Order form

Order No.: _____

Order Date : ___ / ___ / ___

Customer Details

Name : _____

Address : _____

_____

Email : _____ @ _____ Phone : _____

Order Details - Description	Quantity	Unit Price	Total

Started ☐

Done ☐

Shipped ☐

Notes _____
_____
_____

Shipping Details

Price

Shipping Method : _____

Date Shipped : _____

Tracking# : _____

Date : _____

Subtotal : _____

Tax : _____

Shipping : _____

Discount : _____

Total _____

Order form

Order No.: _____

Order Date : ___ / ___ / ___

Customer Details

Name : _____

Address : _____

_____

Email : _____ @ _____   Phone : _____

Order Details - Description	Quantity	Unit Price	Total

Started ☐

Done ☐

Shipped ☐

Notes _____

_____

_____

_____

Shipping Details

Shipping Method : _____

Date Shipped : _____

Tracking# : _____

Date : _____

Price

Subtotal : _____

Tax : _____

Shipping : _____

Discount : _____

Total _____

Order form

Order No.: _____

Order Date : ___ / ___ / ___

Customer Details

Name : _____

Address : _____

_____

Email : _____ @ _____ Phone : _____

Order Details - Description	Quantity	Unit Price	Total

Started ☐

Done ☐

Shipped ☐

Notes _____

_____

_____

_____

Shipping Details

Shipping Method : _____

Date Shipped : _____

Tracking# : _____

Date : _____

Price

Subtotal : _____

Tax : _____

Shipping : _____

Discount : _____

Total

Order form

Order No.: _____

Order Date : ____/____/____

Customer Details

Name : _____

Address : _____

_____

Email : _____ @ _____ Phone : _____

Order Details - Description	Quantity	Unit Price	Total

Started ☐

Done ☐

Shipped ☐

Notes _____

_____

_____

_____

Shipping Details

Shipping Method : _____

Date Shipped : _____

Tracking# : _____

Date : _____

Price

Subtotal : _____

Tax : _____

Shipping : _____

Discount : _____

Total _____

Order form

Order No.: _____

Order Date : ____ / ____ / ____

Customer Details

Name : _____

Address : _____

_____

Email : _____ @ _____ Phone : _____

Order Details - Description	Quantity	Unit Price	Total

Started ☐

Done ☐

Shipped ☐

Notes _____
_____
_____
_____

Shipping Details

Price

Shipping Method : _____

Date Shipped : _____

Tracking# : _____

Date : _____

Subtotal : _____

Tax : _____

Shipping : _____

Discount : _____

Total

Order form

Order No.: _____

Order Date : ___ / ___ / ___

Customer Details

Name : _____

Address : _____

_____

Email : _____ @ _____ Phone : _____

Order Details - Description	Quantity	Unit Price	Total

Started ☐

Done ☐

Shipped ☐

Notes _____
_____
_____
_____

Shipping Details

Shipping Method : _____

Date Shipped : _____

Tracking# : _____

Date : _____

Price

Subtotal : _____

Tax : _____

Shipping : _____

Discount : _____

Total _____

Order form

Order No.: _____

Order Date : ____ / ____ / ____

Customer Details

Name : _____

Address : _____

_____

Email : _____ @ _____   Phone : _____

Order Details - Description	Quantity	Unit Price	Total

Started ☐

Done ☐

Shipped ☐

Notes _____

_____

_____

_____

Shipping Details

Shipping Method : _____

Date Shipped : _____

Tracking# : _____

Date : _____

Price

Subtotal : _____

Tax : _____

Shipping : _____

Discount : _____

Total _____

Order form

Order No.: _____

Order Date : ___ / ___ / ___

Customer Details

Name : _____

Address : _____

_____

Email : _____ @ _____   Phone : _____

Order Details - Description	Quantity	Unit Price	Total

Started ☐

Done ☐

Shipped ☐

Notes _____
_____
_____

Shipping Details

Shipping Method : _____

Date Shipped : _____

Tracking# : _____

Date : _____

Price

Subtotal : _____

Tax : _____

Shipping : _____

Discount : _____

Total _____

Order form

Order No.: _____

Order Date : ___ / ___ / ___

Customer Details

Name : _____

Address : _____

_____

Email : _____ @ _____ Phone : _____

Order Details - Description	Quantity	Unit Price	Total

Started ☐

Done ☐

Shipped ☐

Notes _____
_____
_____
_____

Shipping Details

Price

Shipping Method : _____

Date Shipped : _____

Tracking# : _____

Date : _____

Subtotal : _____

Tax : _____

Shipping : _____

Discount : _____

Total _____

Order form

Order No.: _____

Order Date : ___ / ___ / ___

Customer Details

Name : _____

Address : _____

_____

Email : _____ @ _____ Phone : _____

Order Details - Description	Quantity	Unit Price	Total

Started ☐

Done ☐

Shipped ☐

Notes _____

_____

_____

_____

Shipping Details

Price

Shipping Method : _____

Date Shipped : _____

Tracking# : _____

Date : _____

Subtotal : _____

Tax : _____

Shipping : _____

Discount : _____

Total _____

Order form

Order No.: _____

Order Date : ___ / ___ / ___

Customer Details

Name : _____

Address : _____

_____

Email : _____ @ _____ Phone : _____

Order Details - Description	Quantity	Unit Price	Total

Started ☐

Done ☐

Shipped ☐

Notes _____
_____
_____
_____

Shipping Details

Price

Shipping Method : _____

Date Shipped : _____

Tracking# : _____

Date : _____

Subtotal : _____

Tax : _____

Shipping : _____

Discount : _____

Total _____

Order form

Order No.: _____
Order Date : ___ / ___ / ___

Customer Details

Name : _____

Address : _____

_____

Email : _____ @ _____   Phone : _____

Order Details - Description	Quantity	Unit Price	Total

Started ☐   Notes _____
Done ☐   _____
Shipped ☐   _____

Shipping Details

Price

Shipping Method : _____   Subtotal : _____

Date Shipped : _____   Tax : _____

Tracking# : _____   Shipping : _____

Date : _____   Discount : _____

Total _____

Order form

Order No.: _____

Order Date : ___ / ___ / ___

Customer Details

Name : _____

Address : _____

_____

Email : _____ @ _____ Phone : _____

Order Details - Description	Quantity	Unit Price	Total

Started ☐

Done ☐

Shipped ☐

Notes _____
_____
_____
_____

Shipping Details

Price

Shipping Method : _____

Date Shipped : _____

Tracking# : _____

Date : _____

Subtotal : _____

Tax : _____

Shipping : _____

Discount : _____

Total _____

Order form

Order No.: _____

Order Date : ___ / ___ / ___

Customer Details

Name : _____

Address : _____

_____

Email : _____ @ _____   Phone : _____

Order Details - Description	Quantity	Unit Price	Total

Started ☐

Done ☐

Shipped ☐

Notes _____

_____

_____

_____

Shipping Details

Price

Shipping Method : _____

Date Shipped : _____

Tracking# : _____

Date : _____

Subtotal : _____

Tax : _____

Shipping : _____

Discount : _____

Total _____

Order form

Order No.: _____

Order Date : ___ / ___ / ___

Customer Details

Name : _____

Address : _____

_____

Email : _____ @ _____ Phone : _____

Order Details - Description	Quantity	Unit Price	Total

Started ☐

Done ☐

Shipped ☐

Notes _____
_____
_____
_____

Shipping Details

Price

Shipping Method : _____

Date Shipped : _____

Tracking# : _____

Date : _____

Subtotal : _____

Tax : _____

Shipping : _____

Discount : _____

Total

Order form

Order No.: _____

Order Date : ___ / ___ / ___

Customer Details

Name : _____

Address : _____

_____

Email : _____ @ _____   Phone : _____

Order Details - Description	Quantity	Unit Price	Total

Started ☐   Notes _____

Done ☐   _____

Shipped ☐   _____

_____

Shipping Details

Price

Shipping Method : _____   Subtotal : _____

Date Shipped : _____   Tax : _____

Tracking# : _____   Shipping : _____

Date : _____   Discount : _____

Total _____

Order form

Order No.: _____

Order Date : _____ / _____ / _____

Customer Details

Name : _____

Address : _____

_____

Email : _____ @ _____ Phone : _____

Order Details - Description	Quantity	Unit Price	Total

Started ☐

Done ☐

Shipped ☐

Notes _____

_____

_____

_____

Shipping Details

Price

Shipping Method : _____

Date Shipped : _____

Tracking# : _____

Date : _____

Subtotal : _____

Tax : _____

Shipping : _____

Discount : _____

Total _____

Order form

Order No.: _____

Order Date : ____ / ____ / ____

Customer Details

Name : _____

Address : _____

_____

Email : _____ @ _____ Phone : _____

Order Details - Description	Quantity	Unit Price	Total

Started ☐

Done ☐

Shipped ☐

Notes _____

_____

_____

Shipping Details

Price

Shipping Method : _____

Date Shipped : _____

Tracking# : _____

Date : _____

Subtotal : _____

Tax : _____

Shipping : _____

Discount : _____

Total _____

Order form

Order No.: _____

Order Date : ___ / ___ / ___

Customer Details

Name : _____

Address : _____

_____

Email : _____ @ _____   Phone : _____

Order Details - Description	Quantity	Unit Price	Total

Started ☐

Done ☐

Shipped ☐

Notes _____
_____
_____

Shipping Details

Shipping Method : _____

Date Shipped : _____

Tracking# : _____

Date : _____

Price

Subtotal : _____

Tax : _____

Shipping : _____

Discount : _____

Total _____

Order form

Order No.: _____

Order Date : ___ / ___ / ___

Customer Details

Name : _____

Address : _____

_____

Email : _____ @ _____   Phone : _____

Order Details - Description	Quantity	Unit Price	Total

Started ☐

Done ☐

Shipped ☐

Notes _____

_____

_____

_____

Shipping Details

Price

Shipping Method : _____

Date Shipped : _____

Tracking# : _____

Date : _____

Subtotal : _____

Tax : _____

Shipping : _____

Discount : _____

Total _____

Order form

Order No.: _____

Order Date : ___ / ___ / ___

Customer Details

Name : _____

Address : _____

_____

Email : _____ @ _____ Phone : _____

Order Details - Description	Quantity	Unit Price	Total

Started ☐

Done ☐

Shipped ☐

Notes _____
_____
_____
_____

Shipping Details

Price

Shipping Method : _____

Date Shipped : _____

Tracking# : _____

Date : _____

Subtotal : _____

Tax : _____

Shipping : _____

Discount : _____

Total _____

Order form

Order No.: _____

Order Date : ____ / ____ / ____

Customer Details

Name : _____

Address : _____

_____

Email : _____ @ _____ Phone : _____

Order Details - Description	Quantity	Unit Price	Total

Started ☐

Done ☐

Shipped ☐

Notes _____
_____
_____
_____

Shipping Details

Shipping Method : _____

Date Shipped : _____

Tracking# : _____

Date : _____

Price

Subtotal : _____

Tax : _____

Shipping : _____

Discount : _____

Total _____

Order form

Order No.: _____

Order Date : ___/___/___

Customer Details

Name : _____

Address : _____

_____

Email : _____ @ _____   Phone : _____

Order Details - Description	Quantity	Unit Price	Total

Started ☐

Done ☐

Shipped ☐

Notes _____
_____
_____

Shipping Details

Shipping Method : _____

Date Shipped : _____

Tracking# : _____

Date : _____

Price

Subtotal : _____

Tax : _____

Shipping : _____

Discount : _____

Total

Order form

Order No.: _____
Order Date : ___/___/___

Customer Details

Name : _____

Address : _____

_____

Email : _____ @ _____ Phone : _____

Order Details - Description	Quantity	Unit Price	Total

Started ☐   Notes _____

Done ☐   _____

Shipped ☐   _____

Shipping Details

Price

Shipping Method : _____   Subtotal : _____

Date Shipped : _____   Tax : _____

Tracking# : _____   Shipping : _____

Date : _____   Discount : _____

Total _____

Order form

Customer Details

Name : _____

Address : _____

_____

Email : _____ @ _____ Phone : _____

Order Details - Description	Quantity	Unit Price	Total

Started ☐

Done ☐

Shipped ☐

Notes _____
_____
_____
_____

Shipping Details

Shipping Method : _____

Date Shipped : _____

Tracking# : _____

Date : _____

Price

Subtotal : _____

Tax : _____

Shipping : _____

Discount : _____

Total _____

Order form

Order No.: _____

Order Date : ___ / ___ / ___

Customer Details

Name : _____

Address : _____

_____

Email : _____ @ _____   Phone : _____

Order Details - Description	Quantity	Unit Price	Total

Started ☐

Done ☐

Shipped ☐

Notes _____

_____

_____

_____

Shipping Details

Price

Shipping Method : _____

Date Shipped : _____

Tracking# : _____

Date : _____

Subtotal : _____

Tax : _____

Shipping : _____

Discount : _____

Total _____

Order form

Order No.: _____

Order Date : ___/___/___

Customer Details

Name : _____

Address : _____

_____

Email : _____ @ _____   Phone : _____

Order Details - Description	Quantity	Unit Price	Total

Started ☐

Done ☐

Shipped ☐

Notes _____
_____
_____
_____

Shipping Details	Price

Shipping Method : _____

Date Shipped : _____

Tracking# : _____

Date : _____

Subtotal : _____

Tax : _____

Shipping : _____

Discount : _____

Total _____

Order form

Order No.: _____

Order Date : ___ / ___ / ___

Customer Details

Name : _____

Address : _____

_____

Email : _____ @ _____ Phone : _____

Order Details - Description	Quantity	Unit Price	Total

Started ☐

Done ☐

Shipped ☐

Notes _____
_____
_____
_____

Shipping Details

Price

Shipping Method : _____

Date Shipped : _____

Tracking# : _____

Date : _____

Subtotal : _____

Tax : _____

Shipping : _____

Discount : _____

Total _____

Order form

Order No.: _____

Order Date : ___/___/___

Customer Details

Name : _____

Address : _____

_____

Email : _____ @ _____ Phone : _____

Order Details - Description	Quantity	Unit Price	Total

Started ☐

Done ☐

Shipped ☐

Notes _____
_____
_____

Shipping Details

Shipping Method : _____

Date Shipped : _____

Tracking# : _____

Date : _____

Price

Subtotal : _____

Tax : _____

Shipping : _____

Discount : _____

Total _____

Order form

Order No.: _____

Order Date : ___ / ___ / ___

Customer Details

Name : _____

Address : _____

_____

Email : _____ @ _____   Phone : _____

Order Details - Description	Quantity	Unit Price	Total

Started ☐

Done ☐

Shipped ☐

Notes _____

_____

_____

Shipping Details

Shipping Method : _____

Date Shipped : _____

Tracking# : _____

Date : _____

Price

Subtotal : _____

Tax : _____

Shipping : _____

Discount : _____

Total _____

Order form

Order No.: _____

Order Date : ___ / ___ / ___

Customer Details

Name : _____

Address : _____

_____

Email : _____ @ _____ Phone : _____

Order Details - Description	Quantity	Unit Price	Total

Started ☐

Done ☐

Shipped ☐

Notes _____
_____
_____
_____

Shipping Details

Price

Shipping Method : _____

Date Shipped : _____

Tracking# : _____

Date : _____

Subtotal : _____

Tax : _____

Shipping : _____

Discount : _____

Total

Order form

Order No.: _____

Order Date : ____ / ____ / ____

Customer Details

Name : _____

Address : _____

_____

Email : _____ @ _____ Phone : _____

Order Details - Description	Quantity	Unit Price	Total

Started ☐

Done ☐

Shipped ☐

Notes _____

_____

_____

Shipping Details

Price

Shipping Method : _____

Date Shipped : _____

Tracking# : _____

Date : _____

Subtotal : _____

Tax : _____

Shipping : _____

Discount : _____

Total _____

Order form

Order No.: _____

Order Date : ___/___/___

Customer Details

Name : _____

Address : _____

_____

Email : _____ @ _____ Phone : _____

Order Details - Description	Quantity	Unit Price	Total

Started ☐

Done ☐

Shipped ☐

Notes _____
_____
_____
_____

Shipping Details   Price

Shipping Method : _____

Date Shipped : _____

Tracking# : _____

Date : _____

Subtotal : _____

Tax : _____

Shipping : _____

Discount : _____

Total _____

Order form

Order No.: _____

Order Date : ___ / ___ / ___

Customer Details

Name : _____

Address : _____

_____

Email : _____ @ _____ Phone : _____

Order Details - Description	Quantity	Unit Price	Total

Started ☐

Done ☐

Shipped ☐

Notes _____

_____

_____

_____

Shipping Details

Shipping Method : _____

Date Shipped : _____

Tracking# : _____

Date : _____

Price

Subtotal : _____

Tax : _____

Shipping : _____

Discount : _____

Total _____

Order form

Order No.: _____

Order Date : ___ / ___ / ___

Customer Details

Name : _____

Address : _____

_____

Email : _____ @ _____ Phone : _____

Order Details - Description	Quantity	Unit Price	Total

Started ☐

Done ☐

Shipped ☐

Notes _____
_____
_____
_____

Shipping Details

Shipping Method : _____

Date Shipped : _____

Tracking# : _____

Date : _____

Price

Subtotal : _____

Tax : _____

Shipping : _____

Discount : _____

Total _____

Order form

Order No.: _____

Order Date : ____ / ____ / ____

Customer Details

Name : _____

Address : _____

_____

Email : _____ @ _____ Phone : _____

Order Details - Description	Quantity	Unit Price	Total

Started ☐

Done ☐

Shipped ☐

Notes _____
_____
_____
_____

Shipping Details

Shipping Method : _____

Date Shipped : _____

Tracking# : _____

Date : _____

Price

Subtotal : _____

Tax : _____

Shipping : _____

Discount : _____

Total _____

Order form

Order No.: _____

Order Date : ___/___/___

Customer Details

Name : _____

Address : _____

_____

Email : _____ @ _____ Phone : _____

Order Details - Description	Quantity	Unit Price	Total

Started ☐

Done ☐

Shipped ☐

Notes _____
_____
_____
_____

Shipping Details

Price

Shipping Method : _____

Date Shipped : _____

Tracking# : _____

Date : _____

Subtotal : _____

Tax : _____

Shipping : _____

Discount : _____

Total _____

Order form

Customer Details

Name : _____

Address : _____

_____

Email : _____ @ _____ Phone : _____

Order Details - Description	Quantity	Unit Price	Total

Started ☐

Done ☐

Shipped ☐

Notes _____
_____
_____
_____

Shipping Details

Shipping Method : _____

Date Shipped : _____

Tracking# : _____

Date : _____

Price

Subtotal : _____

Tax : _____

Shipping : _____

Discount : _____

Total : _____

Order form

Order No.: _____

Order Date : ___/___/___

Customer Details

Name : _____

Address : _____

_____

Email : _____ @ _____   Phone : _____

Order Details - Description	Quantity	Unit Price	Total

Started ☐

Done ☐

Shipped ☐

Notes _____
_____
_____
_____

Shipping Details

Shipping Method : _____

Date Shipped : _____

Tracking# : _____

Date : _____

Price

Subtotal : _____

Tax : _____

Shipping : _____

Discount : _____

Total _____

Order form

Order No.: _____

Order Date : _____ / _____ / _____

Customer Details

Name : _____

Address : _____

_____

Email : _____ @ _____   Phone : _____

Order Details - Description	Quantity	Unit Price	Total

Started ☐

Done ☐

Shipped ☐

Notes _____

_____

_____

_____

Shipping Details

Shipping Method : _____

Date Shipped : _____

Tracking# : _____

Date : _____

Price

Subtotal : _____

Tax : _____

Shipping : _____

Discount : _____

Total _____

Order form

Order No.: _____

Order Date : ____ / ____ / ____

Customer Details

Name : _____

Address : _____

_____

Email : _____ @ _____   Phone : _____

Order Details - Description	Quantity	Unit Price	Total

Started ☐

Done ☐

Shipped ☐

Notes _____
_____
_____
_____

Shipping Details

Shipping Method : _____

Date Shipped : _____

Tracking# : _____

Date : _____

Price

Subtotal : _____

Tax : _____

Shipping : _____

Discount : _____

Total _____

Order form

Order No.: _____

Order Date : ___ / ___ / ___

Customer Details

Name : _____

Address : _____

_____

Email : _____ @ _____ Phone : _____

Order Details - Description	Quantity	Unit Price	Total

Started ☐

Done ☐

Shipped ☐

Notes _____
_____
_____
_____

Shipping Details

Price

Shipping Method : _____

Date Shipped : _____

Tracking# : _____

Date : _____

Subtotal : _____

Tax : _____

Shipping : _____

Discount : _____

Total _____

Order form

Order No.: _____

Order Date : __ / __ / __

Customer Details

Name : _____

Address : _____

_____

Email : _____ @ _____   Phone : _____

Order Details - Description	Quantity	Unit Price	Total

Started ☐

Done ☐

Shipped ☐

Notes _____
_____
_____

Shipping Details

Shipping Method : _____

Date Shipped : _____

Tracking# : _____

Date : _____

Price

Subtotal : _____

Tax : _____

Shipping : _____

Discount : _____

Total

Order form

Order No.: _____

Order Date : ___ / ___ / ___

Customer Details

Name : _____

Address : _____

_____

Email : _____ @ _____   Phone : _____

Order Details - Description	Quantity	Unit Price	Total

Started ☐

Done ☐

Shipped ☐

Notes _____
_____
_____
_____

Shipping Details

Price

Shipping Method : _____

Date Shipped : _____

Tracking# : _____

Date : _____

Subtotal : _____

Tax : _____

Shipping : _____

Discount : _____

Total _____

Order form

Order No.: _____

Order Date : ____ / ____ / ____

Customer Details

Name : _____

Address : _____

_____

Email : _____ @ _____ Phone : _____

Order Details - Description	Quantity	Unit Price	Total

Started ☐

Done ☐

Shipped ☐

Notes _____
_____
_____
_____

Shipping Details

Price

Shipping Method : _____

Date Shipped : _____

Tracking# : _____

Date : _____

Subtotal : _____

Tax : _____

Shipping : _____

Discount : _____

Total _____

Order form

Order No.: _____

Order Date : ___ / ___ / ___

Customer Details

Name : _____

Address : _____

_____

Email : _____ @ _____   Phone : _____

Order Details - Description	Quantity	Unit Price	Total

Started ☐

Done ☐

Shipped ☐

Notes _____
_____
_____
_____

Shipping Details

Price

Shipping Method : _____

Date Shipped : _____

Tracking# : _____

Date : _____

Subtotal : _____

Tax : _____

Shipping : _____

Discount : _____

Total _____

Order form

Order No.: _____
Order Date : ___ / ___ / ___

Customer Details

Name : _____

Address : _____

_____

Email : _____ @ _____ Phone : _____

Order Details - Description	Quantity	Unit Price	Total

Started ☐

Done ☐

Shipped ☐

Notes _____
_____
_____

Shipping Details

Shipping Method : _____

Date Shipped : _____

Tracking# : _____

Date : _____

Price

Subtotal : _____

Tax : _____

Shipping : _____

Discount : _____

Total _____

Order form

Customer Details

Name : _____

Address : _____

_____

Email : _____ @ _____ Phone : _____

Order Details - Description	Quantity	Unit Price	Total

Started ☐   Notes _____

Done ☐   _____

Shipped ☐   _____

Shipping Details

Price

Shipping Method : _____   Subtotal : _____

Date Shipped : _____   Tax : _____

Tracking# : _____   Shipping : _____

Date : _____   Discount : _____

Total _____

Order form

Order No.: _____

Order Date : ___ / ___ / ___

Customer Details

Name : _____

Address : _____

_____

Email : _____ @ _____ Phone : _____

Order Details - Description	Quantity	Unit Price	Total

Started ☐

Done ☐

Shipped ☐

Notes _____
_____
_____
_____

Shipping Details

Price

Shipping Method : _____

Date Shipped : _____

Tracking# : _____

Date : _____

Subtotal : _____

Tax : _____

Shipping : _____

Discount : _____

Total _____

Order form

Order No.: _____

Order Date : ____ / ____ / ____

Customer Details

Name : _____

Address : _____

_____

Email : _____ @ _____ Phone : _____

Order Details - Description	Quantity	Unit Price	Total

Started ☐

Done ☐

Shipped ☐

Notes _____
_____
_____
_____

Shipping Details

Shipping Method : _____

Date Shipped : _____

Tracking# : _____

Date : _____

Price

Subtotal : _____

Tax : _____

Shipping : _____

Discount : _____

Total _____

Order form

Order No.: _____

Order Date : ___ / ___ / ___

Customer Details

Name : _____

Address : _____

_____

Email : _____ @ _____   Phone : _____

Order Details - Description	Quantity	Unit Price	Total

Started ☐

Done ☐

Shipped ☐

Notes _____
_____
_____
_____

Shipping Details

Shipping Method : _____

Date Shipped : _____

Tracking# : _____

Date : _____

Price

Subtotal : _____

Tax : _____

Shipping : _____

Discount : _____

Total _____

Order form

Order No.: _____

Order Date : ___ / ___ / ___

Customer Details

Name : _____

Address : _____

_____

Email : _____ @ _____   Phone : _____

Order Details - Description	Quantity	Unit Price	Total

Started ☐

Done ☐

Shipped ☐

Notes _____

_____

_____

_____

Shipping Details

Shipping Method : _____

Date Shipped : _____

Tracking# : _____

Date : _____

Price

Subtotal : _____

Tax : _____

Shipping : _____

Discount : _____

Total _____

Order form

Order No.: _____

Order Date : ___ / ___ / ___

Customer Details

Name : _____

Address : _____

_____

Email : _____ @ _____ Phone : _____

Order Details - Description	Quantity	Unit Price	Total

Started ☐

Done ☐

Shipped ☐

Notes _____
_____
_____
_____

Shipping Details

Shipping Method : _____

Date Shipped : _____

Tracking# : _____

Date : _____

Price

Subtotal : _____

Tax : _____

Shipping : _____

Discount : _____

Total _____

Order form

Order No.: _____

Order Date : ___ / ___ / ___

Customer Details

Name : _____

Address : _____

_____

Email : _____ @ _____ Phone : _____

Order Details - Description	Quantity	Unit Price	Total

Started ☐

Done ☐

Shipped ☐

Notes _____
_____
_____

Shipping Details

Price

Shipping Method : _____

Date Shipped : _____

Tracking# : _____

Date : _____

Subtotal : _____

Tax : _____

Shipping : _____

Discount : _____

Total _____

Made in the USA
Monee, IL
20 October 2024